WORK OF R.E.

IN THE

EUROPEAN WAR, 1914–19

ANTI-AIRCRAFT SEARCHLIGHTS

The Naval & Military Press Ltd

Published by
The Naval & Military Press Ltd
Unit 10, Ridgewood Industrial Park,
Uckfield, East Sussex,
TN22 5QE England
Tel: +44 (0) 1825 749494
Fax: +44 (0) 1825 765701
www.naval-military-press.com

ANTI-AIRCRAFT SEARCHLIGHTS.

SUMMARY OF DEVELOPMENT OF ANTI-AIRCRAFT SEARCHLIGHTS, FRANCE, 1915–1918.

1. *Resources in* 1915.—In 1915 the anti-aircraft searchlight resources available in the British Expeditionary Force consisted of Nos. 1 and 2 Anti-Aircraft Searchlight Sections with fixed equipment of three 60-cm. projectors each. These were employed for the protection of General Headquarters at St. Omer, which was twice bombed during the winter of 1915–1916.

It is reported that on one occasion an enemy aeroplane was picked up and held in the searchlight beams for about half a minute during this period.

At this time night bombing by aeroplanes was practically unknown, and only bombing by airships was anticipated, for which the 60-cm. searchlights would have been sufficiently powerful.

2. *Additions, March–May*, 1916.—Between March and May, 1916, the following additional resources became available :—50th (Field Searchlight) Company, R.E. (Mobile), (comprising one section of two 90-cm. lights, and two sections of one 90-cm. and one 60-cm. light each) ; Nos. 3 to 7 Anti-Aircraft Sections, R.E. (with three fixed 60-cm. equipments each) ; and these resources were distributed as follows :—

1 section of the 50th (F.S.L.) Company, Boulogne.
1 ,, ,, ,, ,, Audruicq.
1 ,, ,, ,, ,, Advanced G.H.Q.
No. 1 A.A.S.S., R.E., G.H.Q., 1st Echelon.
,, 2 ,, G.H.Q., 2nd Echelon.
,, 3 ,, Calais.
,, 4 ,, Abbeville.
,, 5 ,, Etaples.
,, 6 ,, Rouen.
,, 7 ,, Abancourt.

3. *Bombing of Audruicq Depôt, July*, 1916.—On the night of the 22nd–23rd July, 1916, several enemy aeroplanes bombed the Audruicq Ammunition Depôt.

Only two lights of the 50th (F.S.L.) Company and two anti-aircraft guns were available at Audruicq at the time of this raid, and they were unable to render effective assistance in defence owing to the fact that the lights on the ground might have disclosed the position of an ammunition train which was being loaded. Subsequently to the dropping of the first bomb, however, the aiming became wild, and the bombs were mostly directed against the searchlights themselves.

4. *Searchlight in Observation Balloon, Somme,* 1916.—During the first Somme battle experiments were carried out at the front by No. 2 Section of the 50th (F.S.L.) Company and No. 1 Kite Balloon Squadron, Royal Flying Corps, with a view to mounting a searchlight in an observation balloon, for the purpose of illuminating the ground. This was successfully accomplished, but the balloon itself was found to be so unsteady that accurate estimation of direction was impossible.

A new form of searchlight, developed by the Royal Navy, for which a much increased light intensity was claimed, was tested at the front by the 50th (F.S.L.) Company, and efforts were made to employ searchlights to assist infantry and artillery in active operations, but no opportunity presented itself during the battle.

5. *Bombing on Somme Front, September,* 1916.—About September, 1916, hostile bombing by aeroplanes by night began to develop in forward areas, particularly on the Somme battle line along the Maricourt Plateau.

Machine-gunning of the roads by enemy aircraft also commenced in this area towards the end of the autumn, 1916, and as a countermeasure Nos. 2 and 5 Anti-Aircraft Searchlight Sections were ordered to the area between Montauban, Trones Wood, and the Somme. These lights were placed under the XIV Corps Heavy Artillery, and did excellent service in forcing enemy aircraft to fly at considerable heights, and in vastly reducing the damage done. Very few targets were actually detected in the beams, however, and this fact is accounted for by the unsuitability of the equipment available, and the excessive local noises due to gunfire and transport in the forward areas, together with the inexperience of the detachments.

6. *Bombing subsequent to Somme battle.*—Subsequent to the Battle of the Somme continuous hostile air raids were made by night along the whole of the Somme valley, extending as far as Amiens.

No. 2 Section of the 50th (F.S.L.) Company, together with Nos. 2 and 5 A.A. Searchlight Sections, were allotted to this locality, and it was credibly reported, but not officially confirmed, that one enemy aircraft was shot down in the searchlight beams on the night of the 8th–9th February, 1917.

The detection of enemy aircraft in the beams was, however, an unusual occurrence at this period, owing to the causes mentioned in paragraph 5 above.

7. *Reorganization of A.A.S. Units.*—By this time Nos. 8 to 18 A.A. Searchlight Sections had gradually arrived from England, and Nos. 21 to 24 had been formed in France. These units were mainly

allotted for the defence of large ammunition depôts then being formed at Audruicq, Zeneghem, Saigneville, Abancourt and Dieppe, whilst No. 8 Section was sent to protect the Second Army Ammunition Dump between Abeele and Poperinghe.

At this period all the A.A. Searchlight Sections were reorganized on a basis of two lights each, because owing to the scarcity of resources it was found possible to allot only one section to any one place, and the triangle formed by three lights was generally subjected to bombing.

The various local staffs responsible for the siting of the lights did not understand their use, with the result that the searchlights usually surrounded the position to be protected, and were in consequence apt to become more of a danger than a protection.

The retreat of the enemy from the Somme battlefield afforded an opportunity of using searchlights as a means of illuminating bridge-building operations at night, and valuable work of this nature was carried out by the 50th (F.S.L.) Company at Brie-sur-Somme.

8. *Institution of Office of Inspector of Searchlights.*—In January, 1917, the Office of Inspector of Searchlights under the Engineer-in-Chief, G.H.Q., was constituted to assist in the formation and training of the units, and to advise the various staffs on the disposition of the resources.

Late in 1916 the provision of a total of 45 two-light sections had been formally approved by the War Office, and it was reported that the 60-cm. lights were not effective, with the result that the War Office authorized an entire re-equipment with 90-cm. projectors.

To save delay, the personnel for the new units was sent to France without equipment, and this was eventually provided, as it became available, from England through the agency of an equipment depôt, established under the Inspector of Searchlights at Calais. The 90-cm. equipment to replace the existing 60-cm. plant was dealt with through the same depôt.

9. *Development during the Spring of* 1917.—During the spring of 1917 enemy aircraft attacks were mostly confined to the Audruicq and Calais areas.

In the former case the attacks were all unsuccessful owing to the improved anti-aircraft defences.

This period and the early summer of the same year were devoted to the training of the new personnel, equipment of the units, and co-operation with anti-aircraft artillery.

A mechanical control for the searchlight projectors was developed, without which the useful action of the lights would have been almost impossible. By means of this device the projector controller was situated some 12 to 14 feet from the projector itself, and was thus able to see the target in the beam.

10. *Bombing during Summer of* 1917.—During the early summer of

1917 enemy aircraft extended their attacks to the Isbergues Steel Works, Arras, St. Omer, Audruicq, Calais, and the Second Army area. The searchlights had by this time begun to detect and hold enemy aircraft in their beams, but still further experience and training were required to make the personnel thoroughly efficient. In July, August, and September, 1917, very heavy night bombing was experienced in the XV Corps area on the coast behind Nieuport, and in the Second and Fifth Army areas in the third battle of Ypres. Two sections of 50th (F.S.L.) Company, and fourteen A.A.S. sections were accordingly concentrated in this area.

The lights thus concentrated then began to work with great efficiency, and in spite of the misty atmosphere prevailing in this low-lying country it is reported that between 50 and 60 per cent. of raiding aircraft were detected and held in the beams. Several enemy aircraft were destroyed by anti-aircraft gunfire, and many were driven off.

All enemy aircraft were forced to fly at heights of 6,000 to 12,000 feet, with the result that the casualties were reduced to the minimum which might be expected from indiscriminate bombing of a large area.

11. *Lighting of Ypres Area.*—The use of lights in the forward area was then developed on a line between Ypres and Brielen. The searchlights themselves were very severely bombed, and the provision of suitable earthwork protection for the personnel was perfected. Eventually, although casualties were still caused by shell fire, the efficiency of the earthwork protection was such that no casualties were caused by the effect of bombs when the men were actually under cover.

The detachments showed great determination and courage in keeping the searchlights directed on to enemy aircraft whilst being heavily bombed, a result which there is evidence to show the enemy were never able to achieve in their own anti-aircraft defences.

12. *Lighting of Béthune Area.*—In the autumn of 1917 the Isbergues Steel Factory and the Béthune area were consistently bombed, and four A.A. Searchlight Sections were allotted for the protection of this locality.

The action of the lights was not entirely effective, owing to the fact that they had to be scattered in an effort to cover the whole area, whereas in this very misty locality close concentration was essential for effective operation. Enemy aircraft, however, rarely flew at lower altitudes than 10,000 feet.

Throughout the year attacks on Audruicq and Zeneghem were continually being made, but the anti-aircraft defences were sufficient to prevent any serious damage being done.

13. *Reorganization Committee.*—During this period the whole question of anti-aircraft protection again became pressing, with the

result that a G.H.Q. Committee was formed with representatives of Major-General Royal Artillery, Engineer-in-Chief, Director of Signals, Royal Flying Corps, and Machine-Gun Corps.

This Committee took evidence at Army Headquarters from all who wished to express their views. Army Commanders, Corps Commanders, Divisional Commanders, General Officers Commanding R.F.C. Brigades, Directors of Signals, General Staff, and M.G.R.A., were examined, with the result that a comprehensive report was made, containing recommendations as to the lines on which anti-aircraft development should proceed. An increase of 30 anti-aircraft sections was authorized as an initial measure. Owing, however, to the shortage of men at the time, it was found possible to provide only about 30 per cent. of the additional personnel (men of medical category " A ") from England, the remainder being found in France from category " B " personnel transferred from the infantry, and trained in the existing A.A. Searchlight Sections.

Authority was subsequently given for the addition of a third light to each Anti-Aircraft Searchlight Section then approved, the personnel being found partly from " A " men from England and partly from " B " men transferred from infantry in France.

As a further result of the G.H.Q. Anti-Aircraft Committee, an Assistant Inspector of Searchlights, with the rank of Major, was authorized for each Army, and for L. of C., with the rank of Captain.

14. *Progress of Expansion of Lights.*—The expansion to provide an additional 135 lights was in progress during the whole of 1918, and the Inspector of Searchlights arranged to form the whole of the 30 new A.A. Searchlight Sections, referred to above, by withdrawing experienced N.C.O.s and men from the older sections in France, and by the dilution of the establishments with category " B " men. This operation, which then became universal, entailed much work in connection with equipping and training the new sections.

Simultaneously, twelve additional 3-light sections were authorized for the protection of the aerodromes of the Independent Air Force, none of which became available, however, before the Armistice.

15. *Employment of First Night-Fighting Squadron, R.A.F.*—In the autumn of 1917 it had been foreseen that it would be necessary to use night-fighting aeroplanes to attack enemy aircraft, and a letter had been put up through the Engineer-in-Chief and General Staff to the Royal Air Force requesting that this should be arranged. About June, 1918, No. 151 (Night-Fighting) Squadron, R.A.F., became available for employment with the anti-aircraft resources in the B.E.F. This squadron was at first used in connection with a series of outpost lights in front of Abbeville, but the experiment was unsatisfactory owing to the fact that the area was not sufficiently extensive, and very few combats were reported.

Several more night-fighting squadrons had been authorized, only one of which became available before the Armistice.

16. *Provision of Mobile Generating Sets.*—At the time when the proposal for night-fighting squadrons was put forward it was decided to ask that all additional searchlights should be 120-cm. projectors. Further, the provision of mobile searchlight equipments, previously vetoed, had by this time been proved to be absolutely necessary, and all additional equipments were accordingly made mobile by the introduction of petrol-electric lorries.

These mobile generating sets are of a complicated and highly technical nature, and it was considered advisable to select, and train as drivers, suitable men from amongst the skilled mechanics in the Searchlight Sections. This training was carried out in France.

17. *Forward Area Bombing, February,* 1918.—During the winter of 1917 enemy bombing at night had been slight, but about February, 1918, heavy bombing began to develop in the Third and Fifth Army areas, where the 50th (F.S.L.) Company, and 14 A.A.S. Sections were then concentrated.

The forward areas thus covered were full of troops and horse lines, concentrated in anticipation of attack by the enemy.

The action of the lights and guns was so effective that enemy aircraft rarely penetrated the areas, with the result that the casualties were comparatively small. In some cases the searchlights were able to pick up every enemy aircraft which approached the area.

18. *Defence of Railway Junctions, March,* 1918.—In March, 1918, when it became evident that attack by the enemy was impending, anti-aircraft protection was hastily improvised for the important railway junctions at Hazebrouck, St. Pol, and Doullens, as follows :—

Two A.A.S. Sections at Hazebrouck.
Two A.A.S. Sections at St. Pol, and
Four A.A.S. Sections at Doullens.

19. *Bombing during German Advance, March–April,* 1918.—During the battles of March and April, 1918, forward areas in the First, Third, and Fifth Armies were heavily bombed, and owing to the fact that most of the lights in these areas were fixed, 14 sets of equipment were captured by the enemy, during his advance.

Such mobile equipments as were available were maintained in action continuously within 2,000 to 5,000 yards of the line, and particularly in front of Amiens, Albert, and Isbergues. These lights rendered very valuable service in co-operation with the anti-aircraft artillery.

The railway junctions referred to above were heavily attacked, but the anti-aircraft protection was apparently a surprise to the enemy, and his action was so much hampered that no serious damage was done to these vital points.

20. *Bombing of Bases, etc.*, 1918.—During April and May, 1918, heavy attacks were made on Abbeville, Abancourt, Etaples, Boulogne, Calais, and Audruicq.

Except in the case of the last mentioned, where considerable resources were available, great damage was caused, and this is attributable to the fact that the anti-aircraft defences were entirely inadequate.

During August, September, and October, the First, Third and Fourth Army areas were heavily bombed, and A.A. Searchlight units were accordingly distributed as follows:—First Army, 9 Sections; Third Army, 5 Sections; Fourth Army, 50th (F.S.L.) Company, and 5 Sections.

21. *Organization of Lighted Belt on New Front.*—A captured German document shows that the enemy reported very heavy bombing on the troops, etc., assembled in the Anzac Corps area in the Hallue Valley on the night of 21st–22nd August, 1918.

The searchlights had, however, been pushed up in front of this area on the night previously, so that the bombs fell in advance of the troops and no damage was caused.

Subsequently all available lights were pushed as far forward as possible, the foremost line being from 2,000 to 6,000 yards from the trenches, and eventually the lighted belt was extended along the whole front and provided with rows of searchlights two, three, and four deep.

No. 151 Squadron, R.A.F., working in conjunction with this belt of lights, were able to destroy in flames some 25 enemy aircraft on our side of the line, with the result that in the end the bombing was limited to the areas in front of the foremost line of searchlights, the back areas being almost completely immune.

Severe casualties were caused in places where lights were not available, but the gaps in the lighted belt were closed as soon as practicable by new units hastily formed as the equipment arrived from England, or by old units from L. of C. which had been replaced by newly formed sections; and eventually the casualties from hostile night bombing were reduced to a minimum.

Lights were frequently in action at the front within two or three days of their arrival at Calais from England.

22. *Use of Lights during Final British Advance.*—The general retreat of the enemy during the closing stages of the war again afforded opportunities to utilize searchlights for illuminating bridge building operations at night, and much valuable work of this nature was carried out.

It was also reported that the lights had been used in the forward area near Mons in connection with railway construction work. One searchlight had been placed at each end of a mile of railway track, and the beams aligned at an angle of about two degrees elevation over the working parties. By this means the whole length of track between the two searchlights was illuminated sufficiently for the parties to work at night.

From time to time during the course of the war the lights were, in addition, used to assist in trench raids and other minor operations as recall signals and aids to direction.

23. *Anticipated Development if war had gone on.*—An additional sixteen 3-light sections had been approved in the late autumn of 1918, and were almost ready for action at the time of the Armistice.

If the war had gone on, an illuminated barrier, four lights deep, would have been established down the whole British front, and it is believed that the anti-aircraft defences in back areas could then have been considerably reduced, with the exception of those in the area between Calais and the line.

It is thought that the efficient sound locators, suitable night binoculars, and more powerful searchlights which had become available, in conjunction with the high standard of training attained by all ranks, would have rendered the searchlights capable of dealing successfully with enemy aircraft at whatever height they might have flown in the future.

24. *Personnel of A.A.S. Sections.*—The personnel with anti-aircraft searchlights, which amounted to some 3,000 all ranks at the end of active operations, was found very largely from the London Electrical Engineers and the Tyne Electrical Engineers, with a proportion of regular Royal Engineers, and about 600 men of medical category "B" transferred from the infantry.

25. *Training of American Units.*—During the course of 1918 over 1,000 officers and other ranks of the American Engineers were attached to the British Searchlights units in Army areas for instruction, pending arrival of the American technical equipment. This personnel co-operated very closely with the British detachments, and the increased numbers thus available were of the greatest assistance during moving warfare, which necessitated much work in moving heavy weights and digging earthwork protection. On return to their own army the American personnel thus trained were very soon able to render effective service with their own equipment during the course of the battles in which the American Army was engaged.

An Anti-Aircraft Company of Canadian Engineers, consisting of 12 mobile 90-cm. projectors, was formed in July, 1918, and rendered good service; and had the war been prolonged throughout the winter of 1918, it is probable that the Australian Corps would also have formed an Anti-Aircraft Searchlight Company from Australian Engineer personnel.

26. *Conclusion.*—Experiences in France have shown that an Anti-Aircraft Searchlight Detachment requires the best equipment, a high standard of training, and, wherever possible, complete freedom in

control of action. An elaborate system of "central control," such as has sometimes been found necessary in connection with the defence of large ammunition depôts, has undoubtedly hampered the working of the lights in action ; and it is therefore suggested that they should be developed independently of the anti-aircraft artillery, as their work in the future will lie more and more in co-operation with night-fighting units of the Royal Air Force.

www.ingramcontent.com/pod-product-compliance
Ingram Content Group UK Ltd.
Pitfield, Milton Keynes, MK11 3LW, UK
UKHW040604210726
13854UKWH00009B/2700

9 781845 743376